Stories in ART

Tapestries and Textiles

Louise Spilsbury

WAYLAND

First published in Great Britain in 2015 by Wayland
Copyright © Wayland 2015
All rights reserved

ISBN: 978 0 7502 9441 6

10 9 8 7 6 5 4 3 2 1

Wayland, an imprint of Hachette Children's Group
Part of Hodder & Stoughton
Carmelite House, 50 Victoria Embankment, London EC4Y 0DZ

Acknowledgments
Senior Editor: Claire Shanahan
Designer: Rachel Hamdi/Holly Fulbrook
Project Maker: Anna-Marie d'Cruz
Models: Rheanne Khokar, Alex Watson
Photographer: Andy Crawford

Title pages, p16/17: © Christie's Images/Corbis; p6: The Devonshire Hunting
Tapestries, Boar and Bear Hunt, probably Arras, 1425-50 by Victoria & Albert
Museum, London, UK/The Bridgeman Art Library; p7: Hmong Story Cloth - Historical
Migration of the Hmong, story telling cloth (pha pra vet), embroidery & applique,
Thailand, Ban Vinai Refugee Camp, 1988, Montana Museum of Art & Culture. The
University of Montana, donated by Helen Cappadocia; p8: Paul Chesley/Stone/Getty
Images; p9: Frans Lemmens/The Image Bank/Getty Images; p10/11: King Harold is
killed and the English turn in flight, detail from the Bayeux Tapestry, before 1082
(wool embroidery on linen) by French School, (11th century), Musee de la
Tapisserie, Bayeux, France/With special authorisation of the city of
Bayeux/Giraudon/The Bridgeman Art Library; p12/13, front cover: The Lady and the
Unicorn: 'Sight' (tapestry) by French School, (15th century), Musee National du
Moyen Age et des Thermes de Cluny, Paris/Lauros/Giraudon/The Bridgeman Art
Library; p14/15: Buddha cutting a tuft of hair, Tibetan temple banner by Tibetan
School (18th century), Musee Guimet, Paris, France/The Bridgeman Art Library;
p18/19: Smithsonian Institution, National Museum of American History; p20/21: Don
Cole/Fowler Museum at UCLA.

Printed in the United States of America.

An Hachette UK company
www.hachette.co.uk
www.hachettechildrens.co.uk

Contents

What are tapestries and textiles?

Tapestry and textile art is made using fabrics and fibres. Sometimes, textile art is purely **decorative**, like wall hangings that are used instead of paintings. Some textile art is **functional**, such as blankets that are made to keep people warm. Some forms of textile art are both functional and decorative!

Tapestries

Tapestries are woven pictures. **Weaving** is an ancient skill that people developed as long ago as 6000 BCE. Fragments of tapestries have even been found from ancient Egypt! The earliest known European tapestries are from the 11th century. Throughout the **Middle Ages**, large tapestries were used to brighten up the huge, plain, stone walls of medieval castles. Whole rooms were often covered in a sequence of tapestries that worked together to tell a story.

▼ *Many tapestries from the Middle Ages show Bible stories or scenes of everyday life, such as hunting. Rich people took their tapestries from house to house with them to make rooms look cosy and to show off the family's wealth.*

▶ *The Hmong people lived in China and then Vietnam, but were attacked and chased out of this country. They often had to swim to safety in nearby Thailand. This 20th-century, appliquéd cloth tells the story of the Hmong people's escape to freedom.*

Textile art

Other kinds of textile art include **embroidery** and **appliqué**. Embroidery is when a piece of fabric is decorated with stitches of thread. In appliqué, fabric shapes are sewn or stuck on to a larger piece of fabric. These forms of textile art were first used when people lived a **nomadic** life, roaming from place to place. Women made decorative textiles, such as rugs, cushions and blankets because these items could be rolled up easily and carried with them. Then, when people set up camp somewhere new, the items were brought out again.

How to use this book

Background information on each tapestry or textile featured, including its designer, date, location and history

This section tells you about the story behind each tapestry or textile

Take a closer look at the details in each tapestry or textile

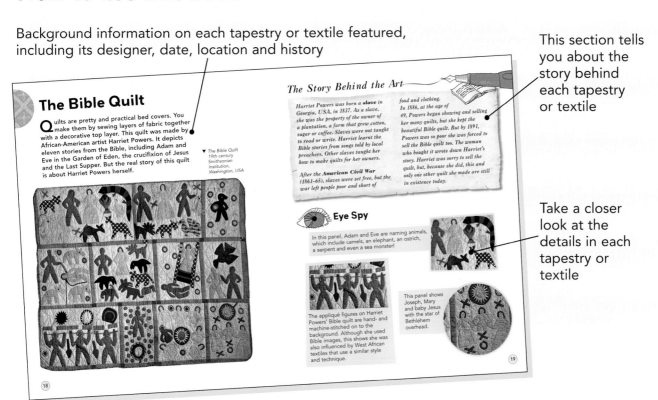

How are textiles made?

Different textiles are made in different ways. Some, such as silk painting, are simply paints applied to fabric. Other kinds of textiles are more complicated.

Making tapestries

Tapestries are designs made on a **loom**, a simple machine used to weave two or more threads together. On a loom, **warp** threads go down and then **weft** threads are woven left to right, in and out of the warp threads. The patterns in a tapestry are usually woven by the weft threads. For example, on a loom the warp threads are a neutral colour. The weft threads, in different colours, are woven in and out of the warp threads in different sequences to make a pattern or picture.

◀ *This Native American woman in Arizona, USA, is teaching her daughter to weave a rug. You can see the cream-coloured vertical warp threads and the multi-coloured weft threads that form the pattern going horizontally (across) the loom.*

Appliqué

Appliqué is a French word that means to apply or put on. In appliqué, paper patterns are made and are used to cut small fabric shapes. These pieces are then sewn or stuck on to a larger piece of background fabric with the edges turned underneath. A number of different pieces are applied to form a picture or pattern. Often other materials such as beads and sequins are sewn on to the appliqué to create different effects and **textures**. Sometimes appliqué has embroidery on it too.

Embroidery

In embroidery, different kinds of stitches are used to give different effects. Some stitches are used to make outlines, like a running stitch in which the needle is pulled under and over the fabric in regular spaces. Other stitches are used to fill an outline, such as satin stitch, in which lots of stitches of different lengths are made next to one another. Other stitches are simply decorative, like the French knot in which you wrap the thread to make a little knot on the fabric surface.

▼ These bold coloured embroidery stitches are being used to decorate a skirt.

The Bayeux Tapestry

The Bayeux Tapestry is probably the most famous tapestry in the world. It tells the story of the Norman **invasion** of England in 1066. The Normans were the inhabitants of Normandy, France, who wanted to rule over England. The Bayeux Tapestry is an incredible 70-metre-long historical record of the events at that time!

It was made soon after the famous Battle of Hastings and is called the Bayeux Tapestry because it was paid for by Bishop Odo of Bayeux, half-brother of William of Normandy.

The Bayeux Tapestry is like a long cartoon story. Some of the scenes it depicts are violent and bloody and there is a huge cast of characters and animals in it, including over 600 people, 50 dogs, 200 horses and 40 ships!

▲ *Bayeux tapestry*
11th century
70m wide x 50cm high
Bayeux, Northern France

The Story Behind the Art

In 1066, Duke William of Normandy already ruled parts of France and Italy. When the English king Edward the Confessor died, William claimed the English throne as his own. Edward was William's cousin and Edward had promised William he could have the English throne after his death. But Englishman Harold of Wessex took over as king instead, so William invaded England with a fleet of ships to fight for the throne. The Battle of Hastings was long and hard, but finally Harold was killed and the English were defeated. William became known as William the Conqueror and on Christmas Day 1066 was crowned king of England in Westminster Abbey, London.

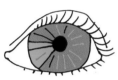

Eye Spy

The tapestry seems to show two possibilities of how Harold died. Under the word 'Harold', there is a warrior with an arrow in his eye, who may be Harold. Under the words 'infectus est', meaning 'has been killed', another warrior is being killed by a Norman swordsman on horseback. The tapestry is the only evidence for Harold's death, and we cannot be sure which of these two figures was meant to be him.

Strictly speaking, the Bayeux Tapestry is not a tapestry at all, as it is not woven on a loom as most tapestries are. It is in fact a long piece of linen fabric with pictures and words embroidered on it in eight different coloured wool threads.

In the Battle of Hastings, only the rich Normans rode on horseback, but the warriors wore chain-mail armour and protected their bodies and legs with large shields. Helmets had special nose-pieces that protected their faces without obstructing their vision.

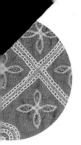

The Lady and the Unicorn

This tapestry, called 'Sight', is one of a sequence about the Lady and the Unicorn. The Lady and the Unicorn tapestries were made for Jean Le Viste, a nobleman in the French court of King Charles VII during the Middle Ages.

▼ *The Lady and the Unicorn: 'Sight'*
15th century
310 x 330cm
Museum of the Middle Ages, Paris, France

The Story Behind the Art

The story goes that in the Middle Ages, many hunters tried to capture the magical unicorn. They believed its horn cured fevers and stopped people growing old. Unicorns were rarely seen because they lived deep within dark, mysterious forests. One day, a hunter spotted a unicorn in the distance. He organised a group of men and dogs to chase it, but the unicorn always escaped.

As the unicorn ran from its pursuers, it came upon a beautiful young woman. The woman reached out and softly stroked its mane. The unicorn liked her gentle touch and was fascinated by its reflection in her mirror. It moved closer and laid its head on her lap. At this moment, the hunters made their move, and captured and killed the unicorn. The woman was deeply saddened by the death of the unicorn, but was later comforted when she saw its spirit in the forest.

Eye Spy

Tapestries with lots of flowers decorating the background are known as 'mille fleurs', which means 'thousands of flowers'. This style was characteristic of tapestries in the Middle Ages and was inspired by the custom of spreading cut flowers on roads and paths on festival days in those times.

Animals in the background of the tapestry are decorative, but are also **symbols** of families' hopes or beliefs. For example, the weasel represents courageous fighters and the rabbit represents having lots of children. The unicorn also represented Jesus for Christian believers.

The Le Viste family coat of arms appears on each piece of the Lady and the Unicorn tapestry. The crescent moons in the diagonal stripe may show that the family has been honoured by royalty.

The Story of Buddha

This is a thangka from Tibet. A thangka is a **Buddhist** painting made on canvas and mounted on cotton or silk. Thangkas can be rolled up and carried between temples or villages for Buddhist festivals. Many thangkas tell stories from the life of **Buddha**.

◀ *Tibetan temple banner*
18th century
Musee Guimet, Paris,
France

The Story Behind the Art

The hero of this story is Siddhartha, a prince born over 2,500 years ago in the Himalayas. For many years, Siddhartha was unaware of what went on outside his palace. Then, at 29, he ventured beyond the palace walls and saw four people who changed his life: an old man, a sick man, a dead man and a wandering holy man. Siddhartha was so moved by these people that he set out to find a way to stop the suffering in the world.

Siddhartha spent six years studying with many religious teachers. Then he sat under a tree in quiet meditation. He did this for 49 days, in spite of attacks from an evil spirit called Mara. Through this, he found enlightenment – he reached the great understanding that only when people stop wanting things and instead live a simple life can they be truly happy. At this moment Siddhartha became Buddha, the enlightened one, and the religion of Buddhism began.

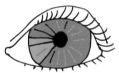 ## Eye Spy

On a thangka, the background colour is put on first, then the figures and details are added. Traditional thangka colours are black, white, red, yellow, green and blue. The design of a thangka is usually **symmetrical**, with the important central figure surrounded by less important ones.

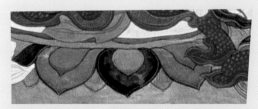

Buddha sits cross-legged on a large lotus flower. In Buddhism, the lotus flower is a symbol of things that are good and pure. It means that Buddha is pure of mind and spirit.

As a sign of his new spiritual life, when he leaves home Siddhartha leaves behind his fancy clothes and his heavy gold earrings. This is why he is shown with long empty earlobes. He also cuts off his hair with his sword.

The Dragon Robe

This silk dragon robe was made for an empress, wife of the emperor of China. Only the emperor and his family wore robes with the five-toed dragon symbol, because it represented the emperor's great power.

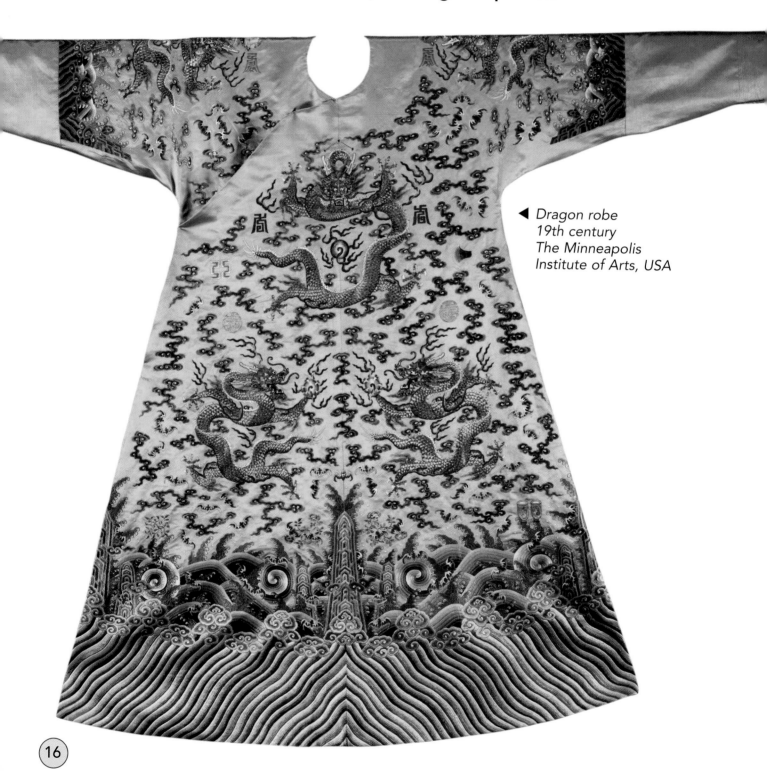

◀ Dragon robe
19th century
The Minneapolis
Institute of Arts, USA

The Story Behind the Art

Legend has it that, long ago, magical dragons lived in secret caves or at the bottom of the sea in China. The emperor sometimes called on a dragon to summon help from heaven. During the T'ang dynasty (618–907 CE), there was a terrible period of **drought**. With no rain, crops were dying and people were starving to death.

The emperor sent a messenger to ask an Indian priest, Wu Wei, to use his magical powers to call the dragon.

Wu Wei emptied his temple of everything except a bowl of water. Stirring it, he chanted magical words over and over again. A dragon appeared from the bowl. It wafted out of the temple door as white smoke. Instantly, a blanket of darkness fell over the earth, and thunder, lightning and rain filled the sky. The messenger only just returned to court in time to warn the emperor the storms were coming, as fierce winds blew giant trees into his path.

Eye Spy

This image of the Chinese dragon shows it tossing a flaming pearl between its paws. The pearl was a symbol of the dragon's wisdom.

In China, bats are symbols of happiness because the Chinese word for 'bat' and 'happiness' sound similar when you say them. The bats on this robe were meant to bring long life and happiness to the empress who wore it.

The mountain, clouds and waves at the bottom of the robe are symbols of the belief that the emperor had the power to go between heaven and earth.

The Bible Quilt

Quilts are pretty and practical bed covers. You make them by sewing layers of fabric together with a decorative top layer. This quilt was made by African-American artist Harriet Powers. It depicts eleven stories from the Bible, including Adam and Eve in the Garden of Eden, the crucifixion of Jesus and the Last Supper. But the real story of this quilt is about Harriet Powers herself.

▼ *The Bible Quilt*
19th century
Smithsonian
Institution,
Washington, USA

The Story Behind the Art

*Harriet Powers was born a **slave** in Georgia, USA, in 1837. As a slave, she was the property of the owner of a plantation, a farm that grew cotton, sugar or coffee. Slaves were not taught to read or write. Harriet learnt the Bible stories from songs told by local preachers. Other slaves taught her how to make quilts for her owners.*

*After the **American Civil War** (1861–65), slaves were set free, but the war left people poor and short of food and clothing.*

In 1886, at the age of 49, Powers began showing and selling her many quilts, but she kept the beautiful Bible quilt. But by 1891, Powers was so poor she was forced to sell the Bible quilt too. The woman who bought it wrote down Harriet's story. Harriet was sorry to sell the quilt, but, because she did, this and only one other quilt she made are still in existence today.

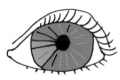

Eye Spy

In this panel, Adam and Eve are naming animals, which include camels, an elephant, an ostrich, a serpent and even a sea monster!

The appliqué figures on Harriet Powers' Bible quilt are hand- and machine-stitched on to the background. Although she used Bible images, this shows she was also influenced by West African textiles that use a similar style and technique.

This panel shows Joseph, Mary and baby Jesus with the star of Bethlehem overhead.

Fante Flags

The Fante are people who live along the coast of the country of Ghana in West Africa. The flags they make are bold and colourful and are used to represent their family groups, rather like coats-of-arms. The images on the Fante flags are embroidered or appliquéd on to a large background cloth.

Asafo means 'men of war'. The original Fante flags were designed to insult enemies in battle or to boast of a group's skill or power. Today, Ghana is a more peaceful place than in the past, but Fante family groups still make these beautiful flags to show on festival days, funerals and at other times when the community gets together.

▼ *Asafo company flag*
Kobina Badowa
1970
180 x 113cm
Fowler Museum, University of California, Los Angeles, USA

The Story Behind the Art

From the 15th century onwards, European merchants used ports in Ghana to trade for gold, ivory and slaves. Fante warriors were known as the Asafo. The Asafo worked with the Europeans, partly because doing so prevented attacks by their enemy, the Ashanti. There were over 300 separate family groups or companies of Asafo.

Asafo companies started to make flags like the European ones they saw, to represent their companies' strengths. Each company had a different design.

The designs mostly show **proverbs** or sayings. They often use animals as symbols of power, for example, elephants or bulls represent strength and crocodiles or cats illustrate hunting skills.

This flag shows the superiority of the Asafo company that owned it. The company members are warriors, shown on the right. Their enemies are shown as vultures, birds that were considered offensive because they live off dead meat waste that they find.

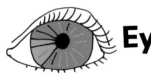 **Eye Spy**

This flag is the national flag of Ghana. Green, gold and red are found on the national flags of many African nations and were used on many ancient African flags. The five-pointed star in the middle is a symbol of African people working together to gain independence from European countries that once ruled over them.

The rifles around the vultures' necks show that these birds are meant to represent the Asafo company's rivals. These kinds of images were meant to insult rivals.

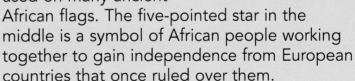

These words say 'All our enemies are vultures' in Twi, one of the major languages spoken in Ghana. The words are written using Roman letters and this reflects the Asafo people's interaction with Europeans.

Print a pattern

You will need:
piece of thick card or a wooden block • pen • glue • ball of string • fabric paint • piece of plain white or cream fabric, such as calico • roller or paintbrush

What you do:

1 Draw a simple design on the card or wooden block. Just draw the outline, you don't need to colour it in. Perhaps you could use nature for your inspiration; for example, you could draw the outline of a leaf shape.

2 Now, carefully paint glue over the lines of your outline and stick string over the pen lines. You have created a printing block.

3 Use a roller or paintbrush to apply fabric paint to the string. Then, press the printing block on to the piece of fabric.

4 Repeat to make an interesting pattern.

Top Tip!
You could make a piece of printed cloth large enough to make a cushion cover, purse, bag or a curtain for a book corner!

Make a Fante flag

Think of a proverb or saying that could decorate a flag, or a symbol to represent your class or illustrate a class event, such as sports day.

1 Draw your design on to paper. Cut out the sections of the paper to make the pattern.

2 Pin the paper pattern pieces on to the pieces of brightly coloured felt. Then carefully cut out the felt around the pattern pieces.

3 Sew or glue extra pieces of fabric or sequins and beads on to the felt for decoration. You could also add some decorative stitching to add details to your patterns.

4 Fix the finished felt designs on to a big felt or fabric flag or banner using a running stitch (see page 25) or glue.

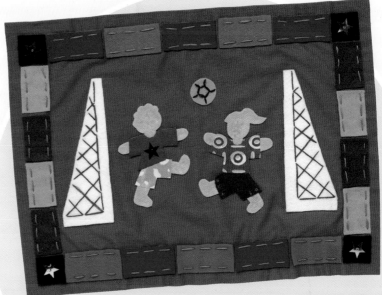

23

Make a dreamcoat

In the Bible, Joseph's multicoloured coat shows that he is his father's favourite. This favouritism, together with his dreams of greatness, get him into trouble with his brothers, who sell him into slavery. After a series of adventures, Joseph's gift for interpreting dreams finally brings him great power, and he is reunited with his family.

Why not work with friends or some classmates to make your own dreamcoat?

You will need:
measuring tape
• fabric – large pieces and scraps • sewing machine • computer
• pencil and paper • pins
• glue • safety scissors
• needle and threads
• sequins

What you do:

1 Make a simple open 'coat' by taking a large shirt and carefully cutting off the collar and cuffs.

Top Tip!
If you want your coat to be longer, sew or glue on some material to the bottom.

2 Using a computer graphics program, design a pattern for the coat and print it out. Use brightly coloured, repeating patterns and make sure you design a back and a front. If you don't have a computer available, just sketch out your design with a pencil.

3 Use a photocopier to enlarge the design and use this to make copies of the patterns.

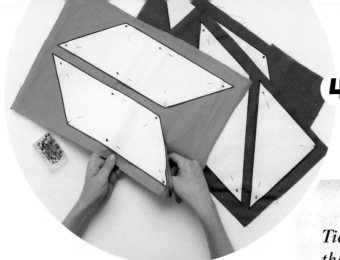

4 Pin the paper patterns on to scraps of different coloured fabric and cut around them.

How to sew a running stitch

Tie a knot in one end of your thread and feed the other end through the eye of the needle. Hold the fabric pattern over the shirt and, starting at a corner or an edge, push your needle up through the two layers of material from underneath. Pull the thread all the way through until it stops at the knot. Then place your needle approximately 0.5cm along the edge of the fabric and push it down through the two layers of fabric. Repeat this simple 'up and over' stitch until you come to an edge or are back at your first stitch. When you are ready to finish, tie a knot in the thread underneath the fabric and cut off the thread above the knot.

5 Use a variety of techniques, such as stitching, stapling, gluing and taping, to join the fabric pieces to the coat.

6 When you have finshed decorating your coat, it is ready to wear!

Weave your own tapestry

Make a loom and weave your own simple tapestry.

1 Remove the lid from the shoe box and, using a ruler and pen, make marks at 1cm intervals along opposite sides of the top of the box. Cut slits approximately 0.5cm long at each of the markings.

2 Now start making the warp (length-wise threads). Fix the loose end of the wool ball to the side of the box with a piece of sticky tape. Then wrap the wool (your warp thread) around the box, passing it through the slits at the top of the box and pulling the warp threads tight each time.

3 When you have lines of wool across the whole of the box top, cut the wool thread and stick the end of it to the box with more sticky tape. This is your loom.

4 Now you're ready to start weaving. Take a long piece of coloured wool and tie one end to the warp thread on the bottom-left hand side of the box. Working from left to right, pull the loose end of this wool under the first warp string, then over the second string. Weave under the following string, then over the next. Repeat this until you have woven across all the strings.

5 Now turn and make the second row of your tapestry by weaving in the opposite direction. It's important to make sure that you go over the strings you went under on the first row, and under the strings you went over.

Top Tip!
Be careful not to pull the string too loose or too tight when turning the low end. After each row of weft threading, use your finger or a fork to pull the weft row into a straight, neat line across the loom.

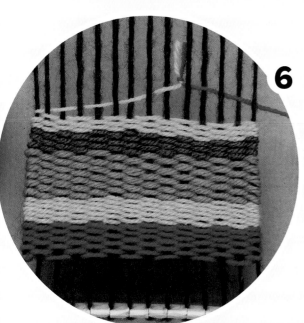

6 To change colours, simply tie the new colour wool to the end of the old colour wool and push the knot into the back of the weaving so it won't show. You can change colour at the end of a row or in the middle.

7 When you have finished your tapestry, cut the warp threads as close to the edge of the box as you can. You can tie these together in pairs to create a tassled effect, if you like.

Glossary

American Civil War war between the north and south of the USA, partly about whether or not slavery should be abolished

appliqué cutout decoration sewn on to a larger piece of material

Buddha means 'Enlightened One'. Buddha is the founder of the religion of Buddhism

Buddhist relating to the Buddhist religion

decorative describes something which looks attractive rather than serves any useful purpose

drought an unusually long period with little or no rainfall

embroidery decorating fabric or other materials by stitching strands of thread or yarn with a needle

functional describes something useful

invasion when an army enters another country in order to conquer and take control of that country

loom machine used for weaving yarn into a textile, such as a rug or blanket

Middle Ages European period of history between 500 and 1500 CE sometimes called the Medieval times

nomadic type of people with no permanent home. They frequently move from one location to another in search of food

proverb a short saying that gives advice or tells a truth about human behaviour in an easy-to-remember form

slave person who is owned by someone else and has to work for them without pay

symbol something which stands for or represents something else

symmetrical having each side the same. For example, the two sides of our faces are usually symmetrical

texture the feel or appearance of a material, for example, smooth or rough

warp the yarn or thread that goes vertically (lengthways) on a loom

weaving making textiles by interlacing two or more sets of yarns together, usually on a loom

weft the yarn or thread that goes horizontally (crossways) a loom

Find out more

Books to read

Arts Alive: What Are Textiles? by Ruth Thomson (Franklin Watts, 2004)

Artists at Work: Textile Artists by Cheryl Jakab (Macmillan Education Australia, 2006)

Art from Fabric by Gillian Chapman (Hodder Wayland, 2005)

Designer Appliqué (Mini Maestro series), (Top That Publishing, 2001)

Science Files: Textiles by Steve Parker (Heinemann Library, 2002)

World Crafts: Textiles by Meryl Doney (Franklin Watts, 1998)

Websites to visit

www.coatscrafts.co.uk/crafts has a variety of crafts and projects you can try.

At www.lazymay.com/sew, you can see examples of different sewing stitches and learn how to do them.

At www.teachingideas.co.uk/dt/weaving.htm, there is a fun activity where you can try weaving with lolly sticks!

See the full Bayeux Tapestry at www.hastings1066.com/baythumb.shtml.

At the website of the Metropolitan Museum, New York, you can see a series of beautiful series of unicorn tapestries: www.metmuseum.org/explore/Unicorn/unicorn_splash.htm.

At www.lovetosew.com/makeeasypiecedquilt.htm, you can learn how to make a simple quilt.

Places to go

The Victoria and Albert Museum in London is home to some magnificent tapestries, including the 15th century Devonshire Hunting Tapestries, wall-hangings and textiles such as carpets.

At the Burrell Collection, Pollok Country Park, Glasgow, Scotland there is an important collection of tapestries in the Tapestry Gallery.

You can see some tapestries from ancient Egypt and modern textiles, such as a woven hammock from Africa, in the British Museum in London. There are also artefacts used for early spinning or weaving.

At the American Museum in Bath, there is a textile room displaying American quilts.

At the Pitt Rivers Museum, Oxford, there are a variety of textiles, such as colourful native American and Nigerian gowns and cloths from India.

Index

Photos or pictures are shown below in bold, **like this**.